Journey to the heart
(*Poetry*)

By:
Rukhsora Lukhmonova

© Taemeer Publications LLC
Journey to the heart *(Poetry)*
by: Rukhsora Lukhmonova
Edition: August '2023
Publisher:
Taemeer Publications LLC (Michigan, USA / Hyderabad, India)

© Taemeer Publications

Book	:	Journey to the heart *(Poetry)*
Author	:	Rukhsora Lukhmonova
Publisher	:	Taemeer Publications
Year	:	'2023
Pages	:	48
Title Design	:	*Taemeer Web Design*

Contents

1	To my heart	5
2	My rain	7
3	My soul	8
4	Turn off the light	10
5	I miss you at night	12
6	Join the evening	14
7	Look at me as a sin	16
8	Homeland	17
9	My heart is broken	18
10	Long last	19
11	You can't be alone forever	20
12	To Autumns	21
13	Hope	22
14	Hot drop	23
15	Mirror	24
16	Love	25
17	This morning	26
18	I'm not him anymore	27
19	I said everything is fine	29
20	Only one lantern left!	30

21	Victim of love	31
22	I'm like a baby	32
23	I am that	33
24	The sky runs on my face	34
25	I am silent	35
26	Nuryomgir	37
27	I lost mine	38
28	The fountain of thought	39
29	My eyes look like someone else	40
30	A cloud took over my world	41
31	To my mother	42
32	September!	44

1
To my heart

Don't open the door I'm outside!

I'm standing, pulling my soul to the handle...

If it spills, my endless sins

I'm walking away from the rain...

Don't open the door I'm outside

In the world I live in, stupidity is comfortable.

You are a colorful shawl, your wings are free,

The world I live in is comfortable with irreligion...

Don't open the door I'm outside...

After all, forgiveness from sins is a dream.

Look, my hands are trying to hold

Faith with cut off fingers...

Don't open the door I'm outside

I will plant a tree from the world to you!

I can wait all my life

If you dare not to open the door!

There is me outside. Don't leave alone...

I'm holding on to the handle for my life.

Without you, I'm sure I'll fall apart!

Without me, your walls won't shine...

I'm inside, don't open the door!

2
My rain

You were still warm, my love

You used to plant flowers in my eyes

I opened my heart like an open palm

May your rain fall on my sins

My footprints spilled onto your path

I'm ready for a hot summer day

I count my undead feelings in silence

But you left everything

September, sprinkle your rain in my eyes

Let the moisture reach my heart

To get back to my hometown

My body withered like a flower

My rain, I will turn into a drop for a moment

Did you discover a new sensation?

Two strings are tied to my heart and it is long

Then I clicked and exposed myself!

My rain will turn into a drop for a moment...

3
My soul

You hide your eyes,

Please wait for my message.

My name was of one mind

It is also sad to fall.

As far as you can see,

(I have no legs) I'm going to run!

I'm helpless, but one by one

I will scatter my "I"!

My soul is broken

Thirsty souls - waiting...

Unable to say oh once

I set my will free...

I lived as if I had a different heart

Ignore my language?!

Now I'm standing quietly

I don't know if my heart is in order...

Do not hide your eyes,

A pair of rays, shining grass.

Save me from the world

"You are a white cloud with wings!"

4
Turn off the light

Turn off the light

and you keep silent

don't burn your heart.

you are scared..

but it will happen!

an ocean will come to you

you will sink

and you will not die

very far - on your left

something, something unar pale

Oman

the eyes

traces

yes, yes, lily

He had found it for you

a memory suddenly clears, a look

all are equal

the sun

moon

star

even, sin is divided equally in half

you wake up again from a dream in a dream

one is not enough for you

light

light

the window

(reached all)

a little bit is not enough for you (tears)

you will wake up again

you cry again

(seagulls are blue)

the world does not shake once

5
I miss you at night

I miss you at night,

The hair of my dreams

The moon is silent to the hidden heavens

I sent my feelings away

Kuz owes me a lot

I'm walking in your footsteps

As if drawing a contrast in my eyes

The sun came out of my eyes

I listen to the rustle of the reeds

I'm looking for a single love

My mind is Muslim, my heart is Jewish

I kneel with my heart

My two eyes are two small stones

I cry at night

Rest in peace

I'm reassembling myself

I feel the night on the trails,

He listens to the criteria and is silent.

Looking towards me in the light night

Who is coming like a white light?

6
Join the evening

Join the quiet, gloomy call of the evening

Night is coming into my heart.

Huu has been buried for thousands of years,

Screaming... it doesn't scream.

I stretched out my hands, I grabbed the hay,

I hid it quietly in my heart.

The world did not notice that his head was missing

A thousand years old doesn't notice, I didn't have a grudge.

My shadow moves to the throne of heaven,

Heaven has forgotten to grow up.

You can't find land, you can't give encouragement

The doll crawls like a sad girl.

It's a quiet time.

My poor soul is cornered.

Darken my white nights

Who's peeking out of my eyes?

Drops drops in my eyes,

Robbery does not pay! (the edge is polished..)

If I say let it be my sins

Prayer... prayer is nailed to a nail...

7
Look at me as a sin

Look at me as a sin

There is no cure for my heart.

finish me off

Your love sinks more and more.

My faith remains at the threshold,

My heart is a dark night,

Who blew? Ketar wakes up

A bandit buried a thousand years ago.

I will pluck my pearl

To purify my skin.

I longed for heaven.

"Hell stepped on my left leg."

8
Homeland

"Come back or leave"

And emphasis on the word Motherland

If I whisper slowly, my mother says Motherland

A longing, a feeling that fills my heart.

If I can't scream, I love you

I miss my country when my tongue is burning.

If you remind me, the cranes will leave without returning

As if a sound comes from my soul.

If I have a corridor, I'm free to walk.

From the pain left in those trails.

The light is slowly seeping into my dreams

From the stake on which my father's lamp stood.

The most beautiful feelings for my mother

A soul to keep in my eyes.

I measured the intermediate distances

You are close in sight, I am Uzbekistan.

9
My heart is broken

So that you do not carry heavy, do not suffer,

Mom cuts my bucket in half

Years also halve life,

Why, he does not get tired of eating my sadness.

My heart is like dirty laundry,

No, not pure, aya, my gaze,

My sin is dripping

It's like a secret that I haven't told you.

November is haunting.

My turd colors are scattered,

My turd rusts are pouring out,

One by one, everyone wears a robe.

God gives the way to the heart,

I made you feel old when I couldn't go.

You cut my bucket half full

My heart is broken...

10
Long last

long last,

you started singing

I didn't hear, but whispers...

I hid your voice in my eyes

I started humming along...

long last,

you danced too

it will freeze in your eyes...

I "forgot," and you forgot

It came from the right, so come down...

long last,

you are silent

I was waiting breathlessly...

and

shouting

reading

you cried...

(I fell from the roof, not waiting for your song...)

11
You can't be alone forever

you can't be alone forever

you can't be alone with your heart...

water

air ..

universe...

to the row

I want to get it, please look at it...

from the spoils of the spilled

you'll notice that your guard is almost empty...

you wander, from the colors of your soul

millennial questions come looking!

You see, from the patches of your soul

A thousand years of sins come looking for...

12
To Autumns

To autumns without losing heart,

Don't face the ice,

Shall we travel your heart together?

Childhood without leaving the heart,

My hand is smaller than yours,

Shall we protect the world?

Our head is as hard as a stone.

Our tears flowed inside

Shall we drink heart blood together?!

Pray five times to God,

Doomsday is not enough...

Shall we catch your sky?

"You are alone, I am alone,

I am Medina, you are Mecca...

Shall we stand together before God!!!"

13
Hope

A whole autumn has passed!

without you, without care

The leaves can be kissed on the lips of the sidewalks...

Let's go and stay

Towards December...leave me alone!..

My heart is wet - tears flow inside,

Fear my silence, fear my silence!

And one day I will put my name, bear

A bullet without a destination address.

I was in love with the glasses!

Sorry for the winter...

I fill the world and whisper, come!

Your leaves are still in my eyes,

We cry to God one by one.

my look

oh my sin

Don't leave me

Don't let the whole winter pass without you, without care!

14
Hot drop

Hot drop, burn my face

My trip to this world is like a dream.

From the pains and sufferings that my loved ones gave me

I don't understand if it's because I'm numb, dream.

My baby heart, your face and feelings are white,

My eyes are sore, my youth, white.

Who fit into this world, what about us, wow,

Tell the world that we are strangers.

15
Mirror

I froze (quiet in moments),

He shuddered and then took a breath.

hide your trembling, my lips,

I want to fly, I have a cage in my dream!..

I'm still silent, from the depths of my eyes,

The mirror does not find a reflection.

He was staring at me

Who is he? Tss is a silent, vague line?!.

I can't look back

My eyes are like daggers...

I gasped for breath,

Let the mirror dance now!..

I'm going away

I want to escape from myself.

In the mirrors of the whole world

I just bumped into myself...

I've moved away, I can't go back!

16
Love

Love is the Mecca of my heart,

wings are needed

to catch up...

(roar like robbers)

My feelings are pouring, pouring

soft heart,

fix it!

I couldn't sleep

to sleep

If I tell you to sleep now,

no sleep!

Laugh - shoot!

(poisoned arrow)

He reaches the destination without shooting.

I dream in my dreams

cheats...

I have only one destination -

your dreams

Don't dream (I don't have one)...

17
This morning

This morning I'm dead, I'm falling

hold my hands, sun.

when you give your life,

why do you have tears in your eyes?!..

Did you protect me?

shot over my head?..

fall, sky, broken rays

pick it up...

Was I born before pain,

or later?

He dreamed of a white cloud

i am blacker than night...

It's true that I came with pain,

I couldn't help but laugh...

I came to your world quietly

(let's go and shout)...

18
I'm not him anymore

I'm not him anymore, the sky you know

now close to me ... more and more

I'm flowing towards the cloud...

hide it (who would look for it?)

the original self that he buried a thousand years ago

It is necessary to avoid clean feelings

after all, isn't it good?!

You will lose everything that is precious to you

and if not, close to you

free from innocent feelings

If you fill the world and shout

(if your neighbor doesn't hear,

if he doesn't hear, he's a chor

if you don't hear...)

If you hear, you don't see that Bor

oh Lord, to mention your name

did I deserve a language, (do I have a language?!)

or if there is an eye...

I didn't have a step left

the rest is a wing -

heavy, wet as a dream

so much joy

and then you want to cry

this world does not allow to cry...

19
I said everything is fine

I said everything is fine, my heart,

Everyone believed, believe me...

I spilled, stared (where is the collector?!)

You belong to the owner, three, go!

I couldn't tell you (I didn't know myself!

Wounded bird in your corner...)

I'm so happy

As if everything I eat is a dream...

20
Only one lantern left!

Only one lantern left!

Is he yours?

Take him too...

or stay alone.

An inscription written under my palms

I couldn't find my eyes...

Yes, I need you!

From your lights

give me a present (for my heart).

Can't you give it from your fiber light?

If I ask (if I can ask)...

No, first you need strength to grind.

If I find a little more (pure) heart,

I'll go to you

with my little bruises and broken bones...

Accept it!

21
Victim of love

What did I find, hazans,

Is it a purple leaf, my heart?

Kirov is naked and naked

Shall I sprinkle it on the poplars?..

The last leaf is dilirar ilinj,

What kind of slaves will they keep?!

Or the other side without help

I'm sorry without him...

And become a victim of one love...

22
I'm like a baby

I'm like a baby

(to a forgotten piece of meat).

But he also remembered

There is God...

Gado's muttering -

The sound of my heart

(neither man nor soul

I don't understand)...

I don't step

my heart runs.

Farthest imagination

on a quiet street...

Imagination, even

from the trembling of the heart...

Not liking each other

live two...

My hand is shaking, I can't hold it,

The heart flows when it is filled with sadness...

23
I am that

I wanted to run over your eyes,

Will you take care of me?

The sand is like a lost drop of water

Is it enough, stranger, sleep on me?

Don't you know, caressing your faces at night,

I am the wind that wakes up your hair.

Telling tales of love in your ear,

Raise your eyelids.

I lost that silent love to fate,

He sought the fault in himself and not in others.

That's me, slipping down the street

He wanted to see once and then go.

I am the bird that smacked itself on the mirror,

The secret dream that distracted you.

You are the first and last of my life,

Consciousness connected to different dreams...

(I found myself in that self...)

24
The sky runs on my face

The sky runs on my face,

Armon reads the verse from the eyes.

Stones flowed from my eyes,

I finally ran away from myself.

I fell apart and put myself back together

I'm sorry I don't have legs.

God says in a dumb language,

My baby soul is a pen to sleep.

My hair is full of years,

Delusional imagination.

Throwing myself away

I wanted to find a piece of happiness.

My face runs on the ground,

You did not find guidance from the eyes.

Wave to everyone slowly,

"Finally I'm in my own right!"

25
I am silent

I am silent, the words spilled from my tongue,

I'm sick, my body is burning grass.

I am a tree, taller than the sky,

Sahraman, the springs are slowly flowing...

Bathed in his age

I mean, stone news is a soft thing.

His hands are hanging in the air

I pray for those who don't know...

At the moment...

A spark, a moment,

Grass born from lightning.

He hit himself in the sky

I am a bird with boundless wings

Other

A fantasy that is brought to the light of the worlds

A tear that flowed from the air crack

The water filled by the mug is colored

An eyebrow made for the day

The moment, the moment came, that moment is gone

The rest you seek from the sun

I'm on the grass, waiting for the morning

That's all that extends the life of the moment

A moment, a flash, the very last moment...

26
Nuryomgir

My heart goes out to you

You smell it without noticing it.

You hold an umbrella in your hand,

My feelings are shaking...

In a lost world

Don't realize it's true

You go carelessly, quietly,

While shaking from the rain...

Your mind will merge

I have very little left.

I wake up in the morning,

Joynamaz is overflowing...

I will reward you...

27
I lost mine

I lost mine

My religious heart is full.

Clear thoughts, illuminated poems

Let them breathe easy...

Like the eyes of a strange bird

I look at my poems.

If I can't write, if I can't write

What's the point of deceiving my lover?!

Sticking a cane in my lame stanzas,

I have a daughter who is a poet, I am proud of it.

I really can't write poetry,

I want to say so much...

28
The fountain of thought

The fountain of thought shines,

In the shadow of the cornered soul.

When I follow your footsteps,

At the end of another thousand years.

A new millennium begins,

In the arms of the moment.

My senses wander,

In the wings of my heart.

The airy universe,

Happiness and pain together.

Toss, collect, re-bot,

I collected it, paid my life.

As far as I can

How many fractures did I get?

On my lips, my youth,

Where is my line?

Cry now, Lord...

29
My eyes look like someone else

My eyes look like someone else's

white in my soul is not like me!

I was drowning in other eyes

Every day, (every day) deeper.

Clouds go wild everywhere,

A light falls far from me...

Did I want the quilts?

Paint when it escapes my eyes.

I couldn't help myself!

This night also passed without sun.

a new seed in my heart

Is it a thorn or a flower...

the white in my soul is not like me...

30
A cloud took over my world

A cloud took over my world,

I have one color in my eyes - black.

He didn't give away his whites!

Am I out of the blue, mom?!

Between heaven and earth

You took my mind...

He did not let him go to heaven

Have I fallen far from the stars?

I can't hear myself

I drove away my dream.

When I cry, my eyes burn

Am I far from Oman?!

The people of creation are close to God,

They said. am i wrong

I can't write a poem!

Have I moved away from God???

31
To my mother

Spring begins with your eyebrows,

You are laughing with your hands folded.

Slowly hiding the silver of your hair:

"Now in old age," - you twist the word...

I know, my spring, my munis mushfig,

Raising four girls is not easy.

Four thoughts, four worries, four flowers

Your mind will be busy with your thoughts...

I have no rest during the day and at night

Who will comfort your heart, your pains?

Mom, can I stroke your hands?

Sleep on my lap...(quiet, quiet like me)

Take to the streets with daddy

I will do your laundry myself.

Don't think about me, I'll do it myself

If I eat just one egg, I will be full.

Today is spring, the season of renewal,

Put on a new shirt, stand up brave!

Don't think about us, don't think about the price...

We'll find our way, mother...

Spring starts from your eyebrows,

Mom, I will squeeze tumors.

talk to me break your heart

I will pick your sorrows from your heart!..

Spring begins from your heart!

32
September!

Your leaves are still green...

But it's not spring, it's a delusion.

Nature plays a joke on my heart,

I'll smile as if you're crazy...

But not easy!

What I wanted, what I added,

Your footprints are silent on my paths.

What did you want, what did you add?

You were quiet on the green road.

I'm not right either!

September! Your rains are still unknown,

My eyes do not know their place...

Maybe you don't believe, maybe you don't know

Go to the autumn sky, my star!

But I am not God!

You want to sound charming,

You want melodious sounds...

In the arms of the fallen autumn

I used to beat my dumb heart...

Sorry, no sound!

Lukhmonova Rukhsora, the daughter of Habibullo was born on March 2, 2001 in the village of Beshterak, Kitab district, Kashkadarya region. Currently, she is a student of Uzbek language and literature at Shahrisabz State Pedagogical Institute and Navoi scholarship holder. Her scientific articles and poems have been published in national and international magazines and anthologies.

www.ingramcontent.com/pod-product-compliance
Lightning Source LLC
LaVergne TN
LVHW010414070526
838199LV00064B/5296